POP CULTURE BIOS
SUPER SINGERS

BEYONCÉ

R & B SUPERSTAR

ELAINE LANDAU

Lerner Publications Company

MINNEAPOLIS

Lerner Publications Company
A division of Lerner Publishing Group, Inc.
241 First Avenue North
Minneapolis, MN 55401 U.S.A.

Website address: www.lernerbooks.com

Library of Congress Cataloging-in-Publication Data

Landau, Elaine.
    Beyoncé : R & B Superstar / by Elaine Landau.
        pages cm — (Pop Culture Bios: Super Singers)
    Includes index.
    ISBN 978-0-7613-4147-5 (lib. bdg. : alk. paper)
    1. Beyoncé, 1981—Juvenile literature. 2. Rhythm and blues
musicians—United States—Biography—Juvenile literature.
3. Singers—United States—Biography—Juvenile literature.
I. Title.
ML3930.K66L36 2013
782.42164092—dc23 [B]   2012000144

Manufactured in the United States of America
1 – PP – 7/15/12

INTRODUCTION

Beyoncé performs at the Grammys in 2010.

The night of January 31, 2010, was an exciting one for music fans. The 52nd Annual Grammy Awards were on! Millions of viewers sat glued to their TV sets. One question was on their minds: who would take home the top awards?

A gorgeous young female singer was a fav. People loved her rich, smooth sound. The *New York Times* described her voice as "velvety yet tart."

This singer's sweet success was no accident. As a child, she'd spent tons of time practicing her art. Now she felt completely sure of herself. The talented celeb didn't just sing, either. She also danced and acted. Plus, she was beloved by everyone! Boys dreamed of dating her. Girls wanted to be like her. People know her by just her first name. She's Beyoncé!

Beyoncé rocks the red carpet at the 52nd Annual Grammy Awards.

That night at the Grammies, Beyoncé—or Bee, as her family and friends call her—did really well. She took home six Grammy Awards—a record for a female artist. It seemed too good to be true. But it was real.

Beyoncé accepts one of her six Grammy Awards in 2010.

Bee knew she hadn't gotten this far on her own. She has a strong religious faith. Her parents have always been there for her too. She's especially tight with her mom. "[My mom] is one of those people you feel honored to meet," she once noted.

Bee's fame and fortune would only grow. Get the whole scoop on how it happened. After all, when it comes to a star as dazzling as Beyoncé, there's no such thing as TMI!

Bee brings intensity to her 2010 Grammy performance.

Beyoncé at the age of eight

CHAPTER ONE

A STAR IS BORN

Beyoncé and her family—mom, Tina; sister, Solange; and dad, Mathew

What's the best thing to come out of Texas? Did you say Beyoncé? Many music fans would agree.

Beyoncé Giselle Knowles was born on September 4, 1981, in Houston. Her first name comes from her mother's maiden name, Beyincé. Bee was the first child of Mathew and Tina Knowles. Five years later, Mathew and Tina would welcome Bee's sister, Solange, into the family.

Mathew sold medical equipment. Tina owned a beauty salon called Headliners. Both were huge music fans. Their home was always filled with the sounds of pop. They sang to their daughters all the time too. Bee loved every minute of it!

POP =
a modern style of music that is usually upbeat

Taking to the Stage

Bee was a super sweet but shy child. Yet in grade school, she took music and dance classes. Performing never scared her. She lit up in front of an audience. She'd often rush home to sing for her mother. She also sang for her parents' guests. Her shows weren't free, either. She charged people five dollars to hear her!

Bee's parents saw how much she loved performing, so they entered her in talent shows and beauty contests. Bee acted like a star. "[I became] a huge ham," she remembered. "I'd just strut my stuff and even finish by blowing a kiss to the crowd." Soon her bedroom was filled with trophies.

A young Beyoncé sings for a crowd.

DID BEE ALWAYS FEEL BEAUTIFUL?

No way. In grade school, kids used to bully Bee about her looks. They said she had big ears. They laughed at her a lot. Bee felt terrible when her classmates teased her. The quiet, sensitive girl took the bullying straight to heart. Of course, today, no one remembers those bullies—but everyone knows who Beyoncé is!

Girl's Tyme

In 1990, Bee found out that a businesswoman named Andretta Tillman was starting a new all-girls' singing and dancing group. Auditions for the group would be held in Houston—Beyoncé's hometown! The group was called Girl's Tyme. Bee, of course, was all over this opportunity. She tried out, and she made the cut. She was beyond thrilled.

AUDITION =
a tryout to test the talents of a performer

Bee (FAR RIGHT) was super thrilled to be part of Girl's Tyme. Here she poses with four other members of the group.

Five other girls also sang in Girl's Tyme. The group was talented, and they practiced for hours. But even so, their shows didn't always go perfectly. In 1992, they appeared on a TV talent show called *Star Search* and didn't win. To the girls, it felt like an epic fail. "We thought our lives were over," Bee later recalled.

It Was Destiny

Yet Bee's life as a star was just beginning. Girl's Tyme fell apart shortly after the group appeared on *Star Search*. But Bee became part of a new R & B group called Destiny's Child. Destiny's Child was made up of Bee and three other Girl's Tyme members. The other singers were Kelly Rowland, LeToya Luckett, and LaTavia Roberson.

Destiny's Child poses for a pic in its early days with (FROM LEFT) Bee, Kelly Rowland, LaTavia Roberson, and LeToya Luckett.

Bee's father left his high-paying sales job to manage the group. Her mother helped with the group's costumes, hair, and makeup.

R & B = rhythm and blues. Rhythm and blues music blends the blues and African American folk music to create catchy tunes with a strong beat.

In 1997, Destiny's Child landed a deal with Columbia Records. The group's first album, released in 1998, was called *Destiny's Child.* It sold over three million copies. Their second album, *The Writing's on the Wall,* came out the following year. It sold more than eight million copies! The group seemed to be headed for superstardom.

In 2000, Destiny's Child was made up of (FROM LEFT) Kelly Rowland, Farrah Franklin, Bee, and Michelle Williams.

CHAPTER TWO

THE BEAT GOES ON

Bee, Kelly Rowland, and Michelle Williams celebrate a Destiny's Child Grammy win in 2002.

Just as Bee's star was rising, LaTavia Roberson and LeToya Luckett left Destiny's Child. They filed a lawsuit against Bee's father. The pair claimed that he hadn't handled their earnings well. They also said he'd been unfair. The girls felt that he wanted Beyoncé to be the group's star.

> ## LAWSUIT =
> a legal action. When a lawsuit is filed against someone, he or she may have to go to court. The person may also have to pay money to whomever filed the lawsuit if the court agrees that the person did something wrong.

The Show Must Go On

Both Bee and her father were upset. But they didn't let Destiny's Child die. Two new singers, Michelle Williams and Farrah Franklin, were hired to sing alongside Bee and Kelly Rowland. But then, a few months later, Farrah quit! With just three singers left, Destiny's Child became a trio. Still, the group survived.

The group's next album was even named *Survivor*! It reached number one on the pop charts. The album sold over nine million copies as well. Bee had written many of the songs on the album. Her hard work really paid off in 2002, when the group won several awards. People saw that Bee was a talented songwriter as well as a singer. She even scored ASCAP's Songwriter of the Year Award. Bee was the first African American woman to ever receive it.

ASCAP = the American Society of Composers, Authors, and Publishers

Destiny's Child promotes its new album, *Survivor*, in 2001.

On Their Own

By then, all the Destiny's Child members had offers to do solo albums. So they decided to work apart for a while. Bee did some acting and landed good parts, including a starring role in *The Fighting Temptations*. She reached new heights as a singer as well. In May 2003, her first solo single, "Crazy in Love," was released. It hit the top of the charts and stayed there for most of the summer. Bee's fan base grew so huge that she needed a bodyguard.

In 2002, Bee played Foxxy Cleopatra in a Mike Myers' (RIGHT) Austin Powers movie.

OH NO! THAT'S MY TOE!

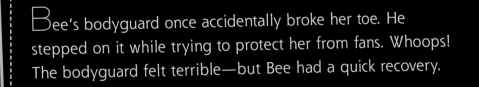

Bee's bodyguard once accidentally broke her toe. He stepped on it while trying to protect her from fans. Whoops! The bodyguard felt terrible—but Bee had a quick recovery.

Bee's stage performances and striking costumes also wowed her fans. She'd wear very high heels; big earrings; and flashy, formfitting outfits. It wasn't always easy for Bee to move, let alone dance, in the tight clothing. She once spilled that "at the *Billboard* Awards [music awards given by *Billboard* magazine], my skirt was so tight they had to lift me onstage!"

Back Together for a While

In 2004, the young women of Destiny's Child came back together. They did an album and went on tour. But before long, the singers wanted to go solo again. They felt they could do more that way. In 2005, Destiny's Child split up for good. But the former group members agreed that they'd always be friends.

As before, Bee did well on her own. Yet she kept plenty of people around her to give her advice. She looked to everyone for feedback, from family members to fellow music pros. "I hate 'yes' people," Bee explained. "Tell me the truth. The only way to grow is to have people around you who are honest."

Rapper Jay-Z became a fixture in Bee's life in 2002.

In addition to her professional success, Bee was enjoying a happy personal life. For a time now, she had been dating the famous rapper Jay-Z. The couple's relationship was growing more serious. They seemed very much in love. It looked as if marriage might be in Beyoncé's future.

WHAT'S IN A NAME?

Bee's fans are sometimes called Honey Bees. They may also be called Bumble Bees. Lots of fans think of Beyoncé as the Queen Bee. On Halloween, she has even dressed up as a bee. LOL!

Bee (dressed as a bee!) poses with musician Kanye West at a Halloween party in 2011.

Bee and Jay-Z have some fun at an NBA game in 2012.

CHAPTER THREE

YES, YOU ARE A SUPERSTAR!

Bee and her mom walk out onstage after showing their new fashions in 2011.

There seemed to be no stopping Beyoncé. The starlet kept active in both the music and movie worlds. In 2006, she was in the film *The Pink Panther* with actor Steve Martin. That year she also released her album *B'Day*. It came out the day after her twenty-fifth birthday.

Bee was extremely proud of her new album. It offered listeners a special message about women being strong. She said that the album is about a woman who "has found her power and has found her voice."

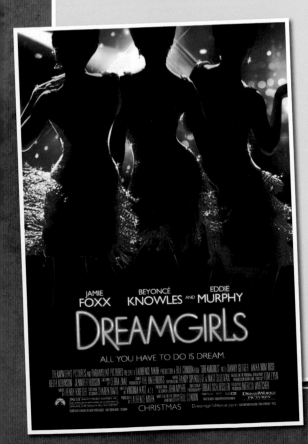

WHAT A GIFT!

Guess what Jay-Z bought Bee for her twenty-fifth birthday? A 1959 Rolls-Royce! The car was worth about $1 million.

Making Strides

Bee was always doing more. She started a clothing line with her mother called the House of Deréon. She also starred in the 2006 movie *Dreamgirls*.

Bee kept growing in other ways too. She did marry Jay-Z in a beautiful ceremony on April 4, 2008. The ceremony was very small. Only family and close friends were invited. The couple was clearly crazy about each other. "We'd been together a long time," Bee said of her relationship with Jay-Z. "We always knew it would happen."

The very next day, Bee went back to work. She was filming for a new movie called *Cadillac Records.* She was also working on her third solo album, *I Am…Sasha Fierce.* The album was named for a persona, or a different identity, that Bee sometimes took on when she performed. She'd pretend to be a daring young singer named Sasha Fierce to give herself an extra boost of confidence.

Bee enjoyed all the projects she worked on. But she was especially thrilled about her singing performance on January 20, 2009. That night she sang at President Barack Obama's inaugural ball. It was an honor she'll never forget.

INAUGURAL BALL = a celebration held to honor a new president

Bee belts out the Etta James classic "At Last" as President Obama and his wife, Michelle, enjoy a slow dance at his inaugural ball.

Hitting the Heights

By 2009, Bee was a very well-known and powerful star. She'd also become extremely wealthy. In 2009 and 2010, she earned more than $52 million. That made her the country's highest-earning star under the age of thirty!

Bee and Jay-Z spend some time in Italy in 2010.

Time Off

Bee had worked hard for years. So in 2010, she decided to take some time off. She wanted to travel to exciting places and do fun things. She took a whirlwind trip around the world. She bought great jewelry in Russia. She had snails for lunch in France. She also went swimming and snorkeling in the Red Sea.

Back to Work

Bee had an awesome time on her trip. Yet after about nine months, she was ready to go back to work. She recorded her fourth solo album and simply called it 4. She also created a perfume called Pulse. It went on sale in department stores across the country.

Is the number four lucky for Beyoncé? It could be! Her birthday is September 4. Her husband's birthday is December 4. The couple was married on April 4. And her fourth album is named 4.

By this point in her life, Bee wanted to control her own career. She removed her father as her manager and took charge of things. It was a friendly parting. "He is my father for life and I love my dad dearly," Bee said. "I am grateful for everything he has taught me."

Bee gives her dad a hug after winning an award at the American Music Awards.

Looking Ahead

Bee's future looks bright. She wants to keep on doing exciting things. She and Jay-Z have started a family. Bee gave birth to her daughter, Blue Ivy, on January 7, 2012. The thought of Bee as a new mom thrilled her fans. They burned up the Internet tweeting and posting about Bee's daughter in the days after she was born.

Bee adores being a mom. But she also wants to keep working. "I love my job," she once said of her drive to sing and perform. "It's a tough job. But in the end, I love what I do."

After years of pregnancy rumors, Bee announced her pregnancy in dramatic fashion—during a performance on the 2011 MTV Video Music Awards.

BEYONCÉ PICS!

SOURCE NOTES

5   Jon Pareles, "Empowerment, Allure, and a Runway's Flair," *New York Times,* August 1, 2005, http://www.nytimes.com/2005/08/01/arts/music/01dest.html (November 16, 2011).

7   HarpoProductions, "Thought for Today—Motherhood-Oprah.com," May 1, 2010, http://www.oprah.com/spirit/Thought-for-Today-Motherhood (November 18, 2011).

10 Daryl Easlea. *Beyoncé; Crazy in Love: The Beyoncé Knowles Biography* (New York: Omnibus Press, 2011), 9.

12 Ibid., 16.

18 Search Quotes, "Beyoncé Quotes." Searchquotes.com, 2011, http://www.searchquotes.com /quotation/At_the_Billboard_Awards_my_skirt_was_so_tight_they_had_to_lift_me_on _stage/230005/ (November 16, 2011).

18 Isabel Gonzales Whitaker, "Beyoncé's Next Stage," *InStyle,* September 2011, 561.

21 Easlea, *Beyoncé,* 13.

22 Time, Celebrity Central: Beyoncé Knowles, *People.com,* 2011, http://www.people.com/people /beyonce_knowles (November 16, 2011).

26 Easlea, *Beyoncé,* 179.

27 Whitaker, "Beyoncé's Next Stage," *InStyle,* September 2011, 561.

MORE BEYONCÉ INFO

Beyoncé
http://www.Beyonceonline.com/us/home
Visit the official Beyoncé website and fan club featuring Beyoncé's music, videos, news, and photos.

Beyoncé: Facebook
http://www.facebook.com/beyonce
Any self-respecting member of the "Beyontourage" will want to stop by Beyoncé's home on FB!

Kennon, Michou. *Beyoncé.* New York: Garth Stevens, 2011.
This colorful text tells Beyoncé's life story and explains how the songstress is taking music to new heights.

Krohn, Katherine. *Michael Jackson: Ultimate Music Legend.* Minneapolis: Lerner Publications Company, 2010. Like reading about pop stars? Then you'll love reading about the King of Pop! Michael Jackson influenced all kinds of talented singers, from Beyoncé and Lady Gaga to Usher and Justin Bieber.

Landau, Elaine. *Is Singing for You?* Minneapolis: Lerner Publications Company, 2011. Do you dream about becoming a singer like Beyoncé? Find out what it takes to make it as a vocalist.

Mendelson, Aaron. *American R & B: Gospel Grooves, Funky Drummers, and Soul Power.* Minneapolis: Twenty-First Century Books, 2013. Read all about R & B—the style of music that helped to make Bee famous!

Waters, Rosa. *Beyoncé.* Broomall, PA: Mason Crest Publishers, 2007. Here's the dream-come-true story of a talented young girl who became one of the world's best-known singers.